VERSES AND CAFFEINE

POETRY AND A CUPPA COFFEE

VERITY HONOR GRIFFIN

ISBN 979-888546655-4

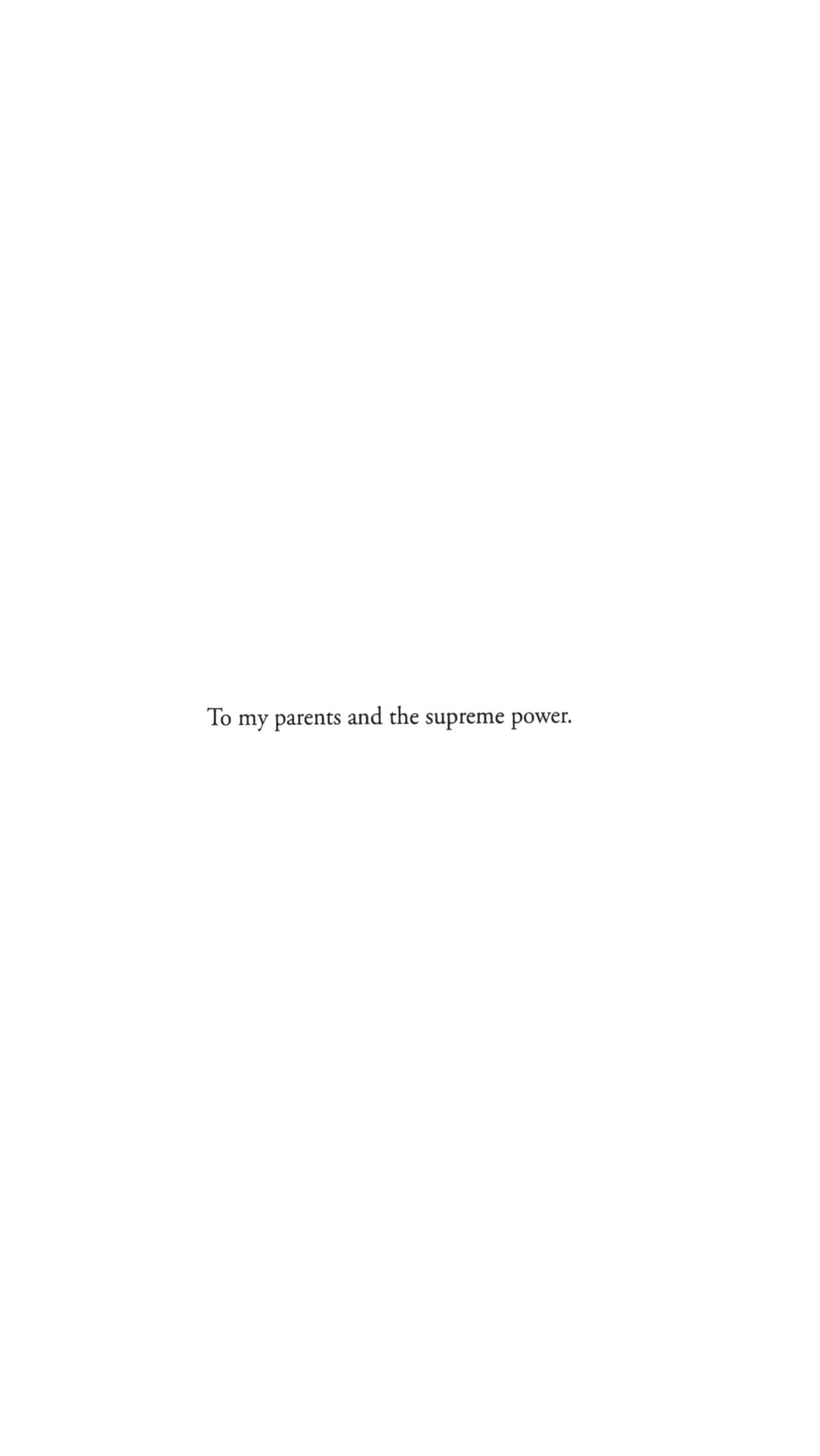

To my parents and the supreme power.

Contents

Contents

Preface

Dear lovely readers,

I am Verity Honor Griffin. I consider myself a poet, writer, reader and a fanatic of everything art and everything as art. I as an English literature student have read so many different writers and poets and their choice for writing and love for the same. I love words, I find words and languages interesting. It amuses me that one statement can be spoken in different tones based on the words used in the context. And that is how I decided to write.

Verses and Caffeine on the other hand is purely based on experiences and my feelings at that particular time. I think this book may be relatable to many readers since it is written based on feelings, emotions and expressions.

Hope you all enjoy the book.

Love, V.

Preface

Acknowledgements

I would like to thank my parents for supporting me. The supreme power above for giving me the opportunity.

My friends, Lavanya, Merry Hart Joe, Paseal Joe, Mohnish, Reon, Bobby, Aryan, Anshuman and Srivats for giving me the positive feedback and negative at the right time to improve my writing and for being a great friend as well.

I would also like to thank my inspirations and idols. Michael Jackson, Harry Styles, Louis Tomlinson, SUGA, RM, J-Hope, Thamarai, Na. Muthukumar and Vali.

Acknowledgements

1. All I Love is You

I fell in love with you,
When I was ten,
My love for you,
Has grown since then,
And when I turned fifteen,
I read Keats, Shelley,
Making me fall in love again,
With you.
This love is beautiful,
My love for you is very true,
Never will I leave you.
I am out of words,
To express how much I love you,
When it comes to you,
I become a hopeless romantic,
Yearning for more and more,
For you are the very magic,
If it wasn't for you,
I would have been sore.
Never did I think,
I will love anyone,
But you changed it,
Made me realize,

Love is euphoric and beautiful,
For it is a feeling so wonderful.

2. Too Much

Too much light,
Could blind you and I,
Not that I mind,
But I don't wanna lose an eye.
Too much dark,
Scares me shitless,
Yet, here I park,
To feel you and your caress.
Too much love,
Hurts the heart,
But to give,
Is not to fall apart.
Too much sweetness,
Gives cavities not only,
On teeth but more or less,
On everything, I see.
Too much spice,
Burns the throat,
Yet, ain't enough to suffice,
Any of my antidote.
Too much care,
Becomes annoying,
But I dare,

Say, don't stop that thing.
Too much friends,
Takes time away,
To meet the ends,
And family, I say.
Too much knowledge,
Overwhelms to an extent,
That I might forage,
To fill my growing content.
Too much grief,
Gives no love or gift,
Of something called life,
Out of which I must sift.
Too much risks,
Might kill either of us,
Yet, I feel brisks,
Of the journey on the bus.
Too much breath,
Chokes you blocks,
Your path and your death,
Comes soon to even talk.
Too much aura,
Gives away you,
For you are Pandora,
I take as too.

3. Magician

I am at loss for words,
When I think of you,
Cause you are life,
You are love,
You are everything,
You are the world.
You bring joy,
You bring tears,
You bring smiles,
You bring laughter,
You bring magic,
For you are a magician.
You, my love, are Life,
I know you, I love you,
You brought me happiness,
On my toughest days,
Showed me new ways,
For you are my guide,
And my teacher in disguise.
You are wonder,
You make me tougher,
You make me cry,
You make me want to try,

You make me braver,
And make me stronger.

4. Who Are You?

Who are you,
To me,
What am I,
To you?
When I stood,
In the rain,
Soaking wet,
From the top of my head,
To the toes of my feet,
You took me in,
Gave me a towel,
To dry myself,
And held me tight,
To your chest.
When I burnt,
My hand,
In the fire,
You put blanket,
Around me,
Put the fire out,
And took me to the doc.
When I cut,
Myself,

Over and over,
You put aloe vera,
And placed a bandaid over it.
Who are you,
To do so much,
For me,
When I do nothing,
In return for you?
When I couldn't,
Sleep,
You sang me lullaby,
Your voice smooth,
Soothing and deep.
When I slept in,
You woke me up,
From my slumber,
Of late nights,
And long days,
Gave me coffee,
And my dose of energy.
Who are you,
Why have you been,
So kind to me,
When I can't be to,
You so keen?

5. Could It Be?

Could it be the fault in our stars,
We meet time and time again,
All of the beautiful scars,
For which I endured the pain,
Only to be stuck behind the bars,
With our memories that still remain.
Could it be the fault in our stars,
That we lost all of our life,
Before we could ever star,
In the movie of "Our Life"
That we left unopened jars,
To create not just our life.
Could it be the fault in our stars,
We endured every single thing,
Yet lost the game, we were the stars,
Of, and became a mere nothing,
Lost in the memory of the scars,
Only to come to an ending.
Could it be the fault in our stars,
Maybe it is and that is why,
Everytime I see those hidden scars,
I break down and cry,
But aren't those the signs, the 'Ours'

For me to never give up, at least try.

6. Elders Know Better

I always thought elders know better,
Seems to me they do not,
At least not as much as I assume,
'Cause I know of the things they fought,
Over, which they are not a part of,
Yet, I assumed they were taught.
I always thought elders knew better,
Guess, I was wrong, all along,
They don't know better, all the time,
But, they act as if they fucking do,
They hide stuff from me, while,
I had to tell the truth about what I do.
I always thought elders knew better,
Guess what, they do not,
Because, they think problems must not leave the four walls,
Of the house, but,
They are the ones who tell their friends,
And tell us no third person should know,
What goes on inside the house or your brain.
I always thought elders knew better,
Since, all of their choices are good,
As they claim it to be,
But it wasn't, isn't, or will never be,

Some of them may have gone chaotic,
Some might go damn hectic,
While others may be laughed at,
Or may be a cute magic hat.

7. Vanilla

Nothing too grand,
Not too elegant,
Not too much, and,
Everything bland.
Yet,
I want it,
Sometimes, to satisfy,
But,
Without it,
Being too much to try.
Enough to fulfill the craving,
Late at nights,
Peace of offering,
During fights.

8. Such A Child

Innocence gone,
All alone,
Staring at screens,
Dazing into void,
A child inside me,
An adult inside me,
Cries, Tries, Lies,
Yet fails,
To enjoy life,
With no worries,
All happiness,
Fun, craze and care.
A child in me,
Told me that,
I am bad, I am evil,
'Cause I don't let her play,
I don't let her have fun,
But what she doesn't know is,
I am not allowed,
To play, to be a child like her,
Because they will think I am weird,
Yes, they assume that I am not matured enough,
I am not grown enough mind wise,

That is why I am like this.
I know her feelings,
I understand her excitement,
I get her emotions,
I feel her energy,
But everything should change,
As time passes,
As I grow,
As years go by,
As I count the days,
To end everything,
In different ways.
Yes, I am a child,
At heart,
Sometimes she goes wild,
And dances, sings and plays,
And lives,
Worrying about nothing,
I know my heart,
I know my love,
I know my life,
But I don't know me.
She is within me,
Trying to come out,
Break out,
Of the shell,
She is put in,

But her shell is her skeleton,
She can't get out,
When I was younger,
Her skeleton was quite soft,
She got out very oft,
But now,
It's hard and strong,
So she can't.

Annyong! Said she,
As she looked at me,
She feared me,
As I grew older,
I seem to have lost her,
In the depths of the forest,
I call "mind".
I have lost her,
She is within me,
But I don't see,
No one else can,
Except me,
Yes I see her,
But she's not near,
I do hear her,
Her giggles, her shrieks,
As she saw the magic,
And the curses too,

I hear her, see her,
Yet can't get her out.

9. Pen is Mightier than the Sword

The pen is mightier than the sword,
I know the pen is mightier than the sword,
But does the sword write a word,
Or does a pen, destroy men?
I know pen is mightier than the sword,
But mightier is the man,
Who knows when to write,
With a pen,
When to kill men,
With a sword.
Mightier is the man,
Who knows,
How to write,
And how to fight,
Or how to cook,
How to read a book,
And how to treat,
A woman, to a nice retreat.
Mightier is the woman,
Who knows to use a sword,
And any word,
How to defend,

Herself from a foe or a friend,
How to speak,
And not squeak,
How to dress,
And how to redress.

10. Memory

Memory,
Who cares if it's the best,
Memory,
Who cares if it's the worst.
The date - March second,
Of the year two thousand fourteen,
The day I forget to appreciate,
Every single time, I mean.
Yes, some may find it weird,
That I keep that very moment,
Deep in my heart,
For it can't be torn apart.
Yes, some may know,
Who you are,
Yet, some may know not,
You are my only bright star.
Memories are beautiful, sweet,
Yet so terrible and haunting,
To relive once again,
Causes too much pain.
A day I never will forget,
A day I wish I had been more conscious of,
A day I would remember forever,

For the moment is fueled by love.
The bright star you are,
In my life and my eyes,
You lovely will go far,
To live your dreams so wise.
A beautiful moment in life,
A wonderful moment for my eyes,
An infant at your best,
A teacher, mentor in a guise.

11. Friends I Can Hold Onto Forever

A whole wide world,
Filled with knowledge,
And a new word,
A new, strong bridge,
To cross the river,
Of the differences,
We have between each other,
'Cause it is the differences,
That unites us together.
A love story by Austen,
Or a war poem by Auden,
Maybe a satire by Orwell,
Could be a ballad by Randall,
Either a gothic novel by Shelley,
Or a sci- fi novel by Tanith Lee.
Also the witty writings of Saki,
And the fiction of Sudha Murthy.

12. Music in Me

There is a music in me,
Telling to be Happy,
For the world is full of glee,
And there is somewhere to be.
The feeling is so delightful,
Always so so beautiful,
And forever wonderful,
Tells me I will be successful.
There is a music in me,
Playing for the creation,
Of everything in me,
Like a celebration.
There is a music in me,
Singing a melancholy,
Yet a beautiful one,
Full of magic undone.

13. Oh My My

Oh my, my,
Is this a lie,
Stayed up all night,
Just to make this right,
Will it ever be?
Heart pounding,
Hand trembling,
Lips quivering,
Sweat dripping,
Body shivering,
Am I so shy,
Oh my my.
Oh my, my,
Is this a lie?
Will it ever be right?
Will it ever happen again?
Is it worth the pain?
Is it really THE sight,
To be engraved in my brain?
Why be afraid,
When one can enjoy?
That being said,
If it makes one feel alive,

Oh what a joy?
Is it really joy?
Oh my, my.
Oh my, my,
I sense a cry,
Tears brimming,
Lips quivering,
Throat gone dry,
Yet, I am in a high,
No not under influence,
But much intoxicated,
Flames put out, quite tense,
Fire so immense, extinguished,
By the choice I'm intimidated,
But your comments so sly,
Oh my, my.

14. Where it all Begins

Mind is quite a funny place,
It is all in the head,
Nothing is ever a race,
But a challenge instead.
Some say it is, Hell,
Some say it is, Heaven,
It is where I, dwell,
It is only my, Cavern.
All the while,
I thought I had nothing,
But that smile,
Told me I had everything.
Mind is indeed a place,
Filled with delight and wonders,
All that I could face,
When my mind goes and wanders.
A place to search,
Myself in when in thoughts,
On the top I perch,
So many times I get lost.

15. To the Best Friend I have

You and I met years ago,
Never did I know, you and I will spend time together anymore,
But we still do, we spoke about everything and sometimes we spoke nothing,
Still you were there for me,
Always.
You and I have known each other for years now,
Every day,
When I go back home I called you or you called me,
You were there for me through every struggle you could see,
You were there when mom was in hospital, and even when she died,
You were there when my sister passed away,
I have known you since I was fourteen I think,
Now I am twenty-eight,
You still there for me.
You and I went around together,
I know I annoyed the hell out of you but you did too,
You were there for me through thick and thin,
People sometimes asked if we were lovers,
When we were only friends, best friends.

We spoke about her and you,
Also everything from the sun to the moon, even my boyfriends,
You were there for me during my first breakup,
Now you're there during my wedding,
I know I will be there with you forever,
Until I die,
But don't you dare cry when I die,
'Cause I won't be near to wipe your tears.

16. To the Friend I did not Love Back

You told me you love me,
Only I could never see,
Used up all your energy,
And never will I see.
Remember, I always care,
Effable feeling I spare,
Jabbed me out there,
Ukase, it is if you dare.
Stifled from loving you,
Turmoil filled my mind,
After all this, I can't say I do,
For this feeling has no ends to bind.
Re-told the story of how we met,
Instead of falling in love, yet,
Entertained the idea of placing a bet,
Naught that I will never regret,
Declining your lovely request.

17. Under an Umbrella

He stands under an umbrella,
Waiting, and wanting the one,
His perfect, beautiful Bella,
Little did he know it is Jason,
Jason is his only fella,
His one and only one.
As excited as he is finding love,
His family didn't want to allow,
Feeling upset, wishing death,
Surprised, when his friends cared,
Him, Jason must be prepared,
And not be the one scared,
Else they will be scarred,
For life, forever, bruised emotionally,
He knew he loved Jason hopelessly.
Family, someone who supported,
Without anything return expected.
"If not for me,
Why for the society?"
This girl too stands under an umbrella,
Not waiting for her one fella,
She loved none, craved nothing,
Wanted to be alone, had everything,

Got used to her loneliness,
Felt good as her own highness,
Expected to be good alone,
"Do you want that in your stone?"
Asked her mother, trying to bother,
"I care about you" said she
"But let me, be one I wanna be,
No one wants who I am not,
I don't want to tie the knot."
"You have to, you need to,
If not for us for the society."
"If it is not for me,
Why for the society?"
She stands under an umbrella,
Wondering if she is really a bella,
Or is she just another fella,
For she is born a female,
All she wanted to be is a male,
Knowing not the consequences,
Accepting others' consensus,
Is she really a she,
Or is she a he?
Bothered her all the time,
Making her feel grime,
She wanted to be known as he,
But will his family agree?
Will he be the one they see?

"What will others say, the society?"
"If not for me,
Why for the society?"
He stands under an umbrella,
Neither being a bella,
Nor the one fella,
He knew what he wanted,
But it was what the society hated,
They despised him, pushed him away,
But he only wanted to somewhere far away.
He did not know who he is, was or will be,
He said "This what I am, I was and will be, see."
The same question again and again,
"Why, what will people say?
Don't you want us to be happy?"
"Yes, but if not for me,
Why for the society?"
They stand under an umbrella,
No they are not a bella or a fella,
They know who they are and that's enough,
Only for them, They don't need a label,
"How can you be without a label
You have to be either man or woman,
Which one are you? You need a label."
"I don't and I am happy,
not for the society,
but for me."

She stands under an umbrella,
With her fella, who is waiting for a bella,
She likes her only one,
And also her Jackson.
She understands her and accepts herself,
Her father on the other hand,
Thinks of her as an elf,
Feels she should be hanged.
"No one can like two people,
It is against culture,"
"No, it is not. It is legal, not lethal,
It is counterculture.
Don't say
What will people ask away.
I know what they will say,
But it's for me,
Not the society."
Everyone stands under an umbrella,
One under blue, one under green,
One under yellow, one under pink,
All yearning to be seen,
But the world wanting them to sink,
One waiting for a Bella,
Another for a fella,
All wanting to be happy,
Only for themselves, not the society.

18. Mirror on the Wall

Mirror mirror on the wall,
I may not be the fairest of all,
But I sure am tall,
Among them all,
For you can see me from afar,
Cause your visions have no bar,
And you are the guitar,
That can play any melody,
Or chords that has beauty.
Mirror, mirror on the wall,
Tell me who is the fairest of all,
It is not me, for I am not at all,
He is, I know it and you see it too,
Because I surely do,
For I really have no clue,
About what I would do without you.
Mirror on the wall,
Is it you that gave me all,
Or was it the angel,
That answered my call,
From up above,
With no filter at all,
And no autotune,

Yes, it must be,
For she sure knows,
How to end it all.
The pain,
Caused by the stake,
Or the hurt,
Caused by the heart break,
The burn,
Caused by not the flame,
But by the blame.
Mirror mirror on the wall,
Tell me,
Who is the fairest of all,
Is it me?
Maybe,
Could be,
Shouldn't it be?
At least in my eyes,
Stop with the lies.

19. Notifications

I send you a text
And wait and wait and wait at least for a notification
When I get one
I light up, my heart flutters
Thinking it's from you
But my heart breaks
To see it is not you
Yet I wait for your reply
Which I will never get.
I send you a text,
I wait, wait and wait,
While I anticipate,
To find out what's next,
I wait for the one,
Notification,
To trigger a *ding*,
It ends up a hoarding,
For a nonsense ad,
That my eyes glow up to see.

20. AnXiOuS

I know that you are not happy,
I am trying to make you feel better,
When I can't do it I feel crappy,
What do I do I'm no great abetter.
One thing, I know is that,
Everyone can do anything,
Just by trying to think positive,
I understand it is difficult,
But you have to try,
Hold your head high,
Wipe your tears dry,
And do it again, try.
You worry, about what?
Nothing to worry about,
Just think you achieved it,
You are that person,
Who you always wanted to be,
You will definitely see,
See all the reason,
You worried about didn't come your way,
It wasn't really there,
It was all just your imagination,
Just something you were takin'

Made you nervous and shakin‘
It is very nerve wrackin’.
But let it all go away,
You will be great one day,
Throw all negativity away,
Your mind will be blown away,
By your doing it a unique way,
You will remember "you tried it that day,
To be where you are this very day."
And thank yourself, love yourself,
Most importantly believe in yourself.

21. Dear Lover

Dear lover,
I know I hurt you, earlier,
But I didn't mean to, you need someone new,
She is the one, who deserves all your love,
Cause she has loved you ever since I knew.
I loved you earlier, but not now,
And you want me to keep you, but I don't love you anymore,
Which is something I would throw,
No, not that you are unworthy, only cos she deserves you more.
Your love is worthy for her to keep,
For it is a big leap,
Don't let this seep,
Into your mind, Cause your love is deep.
You say you want me to stay,
But I must go away,
If not today,
Some other day,
I want that one day,
To be today.
I must leave for your good,
And please don't be rude.
Show her, tell her, how much you love her,

And treat her like a queen, to let her remember,
Whenever she needs you be her chauffeur,
Because you will be the only one she'll prefer,
Be her only to defer,
And make her infer,
Your love for her,
And be her lover,
For today and Forever.
Yours sincerely,
Ex-lover.

22. One Big Step

Taking a big step ahead
Is exhausting and confusing,
Once it is done
There is no turning back
No regrets and no crack
Only once that step
Can be taken for the first time
So gather all the guts
Do it once and for all.
No promise,
It will be the best,
But it won't be the worst,
Once it is done,
There is no time to mourn,
What's done is done,
Don't overthink,
Overreact,
It will be gone in a blink.
It might be scary,
But don't worry,
It might be the most,
Important, best step,
Of life,

And will never be forgotten,
Not all think through,
That one big step.

23. Rose's Jade

She gave me a rose,
Just the other day,
Telling all about her Rose,
She said, "You are my Jade.
I always want you to stay."
"Of course my lovely Rose,
I will even if we are FAR AWAY. "
I replied. Now she is gone away,
Not just from me, but from the world,
But only her body is gone, since DEATH,
As we all call it, is only for the physical presence,
She will live through my love for her,
The rose she gave me and the memories,
We made together, she will always be my,
Beautiful, wonderful, gorgeous, lovely Rose,
She didn't bid me farewell,
For her leaving was so sudden,
But she will live with me in my head,
For her loving was not so sudden,
I held her in my arms instead,
To bid her a proper farewell.
I would have wanted her,
Even if we were apart,

Even if she wasn't my Rose,
She would always be in my heart,
Her sleep, the eternal sleep,
A peaceful, calm sleep,
She had no pain,
No worries No vain,
She had a great gain,
I know she is my rose,
My lovely beautiful, withered rose,
She has withered only to show me,
The true value of her love, and the life,
We all happen to live,
She will be happy, I know that,
Cause she will be with me,
In the form of,
Her memories, her love,
And the rose she gave me.

24. Blow Me Away

Blow me away,
With your words,
With your thoughts,
And yourself.
Blow me away,
For you are amazing,
At every melody you make,
Every word you write,
Every piece you paint
And every song you sing.
Just blow me away,
With anything, and everything,
Anytime, and every time.
Blow me away,
Again and again.
Blow me and my mind away,
In every single way,
I adore you, and your art,
From the depth of my heart,
It is my fire,
My true desire.
Blow me away,
As far as you can,

With your talent,
Your art, creativity,
And your work of true beauty.
Blow me away,
I am serious,
Show me everything you got,
No judgement, only art,
Talent, creativity and your ideas.
Blow me away,
Like the storm,
With your power moves,
Your ideas, and views,
As best as you can,
Blow me far, far, away.

25. Sound of Silence

It is in these moments,
That I remember,
You and I are together,
You and I forever.
I see it all now,
I see it clear, and I know,
What I am going through,
What I should and could do,
Cause at the end of the day,
You are the one with me all day.
You are beautiful,
But I avoid you,
Cause you make me wonder,
What the hell I did,
Back in grade five,
Or what I am,
Doing right now,
I feel a thunder,
Whenever I am with you,
That is painful,
Yet so beautiful,
Just like you, my dear.
I avoid you at all costs,

To be away from you,
And the things you do to me,
But when I need you the most,
You hide away like a rat,
And I lose my mind, searching you see.
Yet, you are the habit that I can't break,
You are the feeling that I can't put down,
You are the shiver that I can't shake,
You are the high that I need always,
To do things I must, and,
To not be the coward I am.

26. Shower of Love

As it drizzles,
I feel it poke,
Me,
To get,
My attention.
As it pours,
I stand under it,
Waiting to be,
Soaked fully.
As it floods,
I feel it vent,
Out its anger,
On me, yet,
I stand under,
Getting drowned.
As it finishes,
The flow changes,
From flooding,
To pouring,
To drizzling,
And the halt.
I feel the halt,
The sudden stop,

Sending shivers,
Through my body,
Even through my heart.
As it is done,
With me,
Leaves me,
Broken,
Into pieces,
Scattered,
All around,
Waiting,
To be put together.
Even though I'm,
Broken,
I could feel it in the air,
The wetness,
After,
The fragrance,
Left behind,
Even the dew,
On the leaves,
Grass and trees.
I pick myself up,
Stick myself back together,
And get soaked,
Again, to hold on tighter,
But I am broken,

Again,
As it leaves me alone,
Revealing my tears,
Unveiling my fears,
Out in the open,
For everyone to see.
I pull myself together,
Again,
Only to be shattered,
Again,
Yet I love this game,
I play,
The thrill of getting,
Caught,
The fear of getting,
Unveiled,
The content of it being,
There.
Yes, it arrives every year,
For half the year,
Helping reap,
The seeds sown,
Before,
As I have always known.
Giving me the pleasure,
Of getting poked,
Of the wetness,

The chillness,
And the fragrance.

27. Certain? Uncertain?

Everything is uncertain today,
People say,
When was life ever certain,
Did we know about our birth,
Do we know about our death,
All we can do is pray,
To God,
To the Universe,
To the Supreme Power,
To Help us get through hard times,
To give us health,
To give us immunity,
To give us wealth,
To give us an ounce of strength,
To stand up for ourself,
To take care of ourself.
Everything is uncertain today,
People say,
When was life ever certain,
Did we know of our day,
What all has got to happen,
Do we know of our luck,
Or if we might have saseng,

All we can do is choose and wait,
To finish a task,
And pray while we wait,
For we could always bask,
In God's grace,
To stand up for ourself,
To take care of ourself.

28. An Artist

An artist is an artist,
Whence he is from an artistic family,
What we non artistic heirs do to,
Create art that we love,
And we want the others to see,
Is often considered ridiculous,
Even in a modern society as ours.
An artist is not only ones who,
Paint, Sketch or draw,
Artists are those who,
Thrive for anything to do,
Out of love, and be in love with it,
Yet, arts is only painting, or drawing or sketching,
But I consider everything is an art,
A cook who cooks food with passion,
To fulfill one's appetite and tongue,
Is an artist himself,
A doctor who saves lives,
Serves the society,
Is an artist too,
A writer who writes to,
Satisfy her needs to express,
And present her thoughts to the public,

Is an artist as well,
A mother is an artist,
She does each and every household chore,
Takes care of the family,
And balances the finances of the home.
So what I am trying to say is,
Every single thing we do is an art,
We must identify how to flourish,
And nourish ourselves and the art both.

29. Ate Away At Her

I ate through her heart,
Her body and her mind,
She was a lost cause,
None could understand,
Why it was,
I on the other hand knew well,
Because I ate away at her.
I ate my way through her life,
Pushed her buttons,
As much as I could until she gave up,
Only if she apologized,
Could she have lived,
Only if she had no remorse,
Could she have gone with the flow,
But she coupdnt,
Because I ate away at her.
I ate through her so called heart,
She did wrong she knew,
Yet she couldn't ask for forgiveness,
But she was consumed,
By none other than me,
She could not sleep or eat,
For I am the one to eat,

I ate away at her.
I ate away at her slowly,
So slowly that she never knew,
She never understood, why,
Her heart had given away,
Her mind had been made up,
She had completely given up,
Now, she waited,
Waited for her demise,
In her old, cream coloured chemise,
As I ate away at her.

30. Believe Me It's True

Believe me, it's true,
I am who I am,
I care for you,
I love you,
If you wanna leave,
I understand and who,
Am I to stop you,
But I merely ask you to believe me,
And be with me like I am with you,
Even if you don't trust me,
That's alright, I understand,
Please leave,
If you don't believe,
No one needs to be here,
Because I ask you to be,
You should be here if you trust me,
And believe me.
I want you to believe me,
That's all, I don't need to beg you,
If you are my friend,
And I don't need to explain myself,
More than once,
You would believe and trust me,

If you are not, please leave,
I don't need you,
I speak my mind out all the time,
All the FUCKING time,
I don't need to explain why I thought of that,
Why I think, I spoke it out,
Because that's what came to my mind,
At that particular moment.

31. I Fear Heights

You call me goddess,
But don't place me so high,
I am scared of falling down,
And I am afraid of heights,
I request you please,
To not do it again,
I feel lost,
I can't pay the cost,
Of hurting myself,
Over and over,
Standing atop,
It's scary, a lot,
Trying not,
To be frightened,
And not lose balance,
And fall off the edge.
I fear heights,
Don't you really know?
I might lose balance,
I might fall of the cliff,
I wanna sing and dance,
And learn to live,
But you place me so high, my love,

I might fall off,
I might end up hurting,
Myself and you as well,
Yet, you place me so high,
And call me your goddess,
That's why,
I love heights.

32. Do Re Mi

Do you know why I love music?
Out of all the arts out there?
Reminiscing the beauty of it,
Etched into my nerves.
Music, the language of my soul,
Igniting a fire deep within.
Flames too big to put,
Away by some water.
Sewn together in my DNA,
Ombre waves of love.
Language of love and lust,
Aphrodisiac gift to you and I.
Trembling in pleasure,
Ineffable in nature.

33. Days So Cold

Days so cold,
Weeks go by,
Without stories told,
Your grandmother and I.
Days so cold,
Months go by,
House now sold,
Ours as called by her and I.
Days so cold,
Years gone by,
We are now old,
Where am I?
Days so cold,
I don't know why,
Is it the mold,
Or the fault in my eye?

34. Sweet Dreams

Good night, my love,
Sweet dreams may you have,
All the beauty may you see,
In one's ever lasting glow,
Up above may you see,
The life ought to have and one,
You ought to forever be.
Good night, my darling,
Sweet dreams may you have,
Good night, sleep tight,
In the waters sparkling,
Is the glow, may you have,
For the sweet, dark night.
Good night, my dear,
Sweet dreams may you see,
All the love you already have,
And all the fear,
Lost upon the night so calm,
And well lit it will be.

35. Scars

I have scars,
All over my body,
I see them,
I hope you see too.
Some of them,
I am proud of,
Some of them,
I am not.
Some are on the outside,
Visible to the world,
Some are on the inside,
Which only I can see.
Some make sense,
And give hope,
Some make no sense,
And I feel lost.
A few with some,
Happy memory,
And a few with
Some misery.
As I cried,
And cried, and cried,
Yet I tried,

And tried and tried.
I cried,
Because these hurt,
I tried,
To cure my dear heart.

36. To Love and Be Loved

I gendered words,
Trying to appreciate you,
While I spoke,
Clothes have no gender,
My love for you is tender,
Your love for me is braver,
'Cause boys don't love boys,
And girls don't love girls.
You are either a man,
Or a woman,
You can't be in between,
'Cause they haven't seen,
The middle or the other extreme,
"What I say is only right" they say,
"Because I have seen only,
A man and woman,
Fall in love with each other,
And there is gender no other".
After all they are human,
Would they know,
What it is to be someone,
Nowhere to be found,
God created them,

With flaws, and some laws,
Yet all to love,
And be loved.

37. Rather Be Alone

I expected you to know me,
That is what friends are for, aren't they?
I did not know you would judge me,
If I had I would not have told you, the way,
I swing, not anytime soon, not until,
I fully knew you would accept me.
I expected you to accept me,
The way I am, my likes and dislikes,
Not to follow it, but to agree,
With me if it was right, else take it light,
Not be so harsh and prick me with your spikes,
Of beliefs, views and opinion of might.
Is this the way, a friend would be,
If yes, then I don't want this,
I would love to be alone, than in bad company,
And take the insults and diss,
If that's what friendships are,
No, thank you, please don't scar,
Me.

38. Happiness

Happiness is not what you see,
But what you believe it to be.
Being happy, creating memories is important,
As well as it is that is constant,
It is not just dreams,
It is nightmares too,
Of different themes,
Which are really true.
You just have to believe,
Because it is what you weave,
It is all that you have done,
And what you have won,
Don't you dare leave,
The world you dreamed of,
Cause others will reave,
What you really do love.
Because this is no puppy love,
It is your first true love.

39. I Admit I Lost

I admit, I lost the fight,
Of proving myself,
I give up, please just leave me,
You win, you are respected,
You are accepted, you are
Great, you are the best,
Just leave me alone,
And my friends alone too.
I admit I lost the fight,
Of trying to convince others,
That I hate you, and I don't love you,
Hell, I don't even know what love is,
Not hate, it's a strong word,
I did hate you, earlier but I don't now,
Because the word is too,
Strong for a woman like me,
I love everyone, I respect everyone,
I love any human being as a human,
Love here is merely, being accepting,
Of an individual, for who they are.
I admit I lost the fight,
Stop giving me a fright,
I can't handle it anymore,

Why did they assume, I loved you,
When I hated you from the core,
To the peak? It is not fair,
When you aren't even there,
I admit I did some silly, idiotic things,
I just wanted to be respected,
And be given respect and responded,
When I speak, I wanted to feel only that,
I never wanted to love anyone,
Nor did I want to have a crush,
I had enough crushes and love,
In my life to be loved and be in love.
I admit, I lost the fight,
Stop, being a part of my life,
And taking over my love for,
Things I love, and people I care,
Stop it, just stop it,
Stop ruining my reputation,
My career and my everything,
I have cried enough in life,
Trying to prove myself,
That I did not do what they,
Claim I did, or what I did not do,
I am sorry, enough is enough,
I had already left you, forgotten you,
Given up on my passion,
Because of you, I am competitive,

I want to win, in my career and in life,
I am better than you, and I am fed up,
Of trying to prove that.

40. One in a Billion Stars

I am one of the billion stars
I follow you, my moon, like the stars,
I am just one of the billions,
That you have in your Army,
And go everywhere,
You do so, to know,
Be and love, love,
Yourself and,
I do,
Love.

41. At 9 in the Morning

A blanket of grey over,
Covering the sky,
For the warmth, and cover.
As the birds fly,
Above my head,
Chirping, cawing, flapping,
A feast to the eye.
Sound of water falling,
Under my feet,
An airplane flying,
My eyes meet.
Far off in the distance,
Stands a tower,
Sending and receiving signals,
From the headquarter.
Behind me, an empty classroom,
With fans switched on,
Footsteps of my teacher echoing,
So did my classmates as they walked on.
A lone palm tree,
Stands tall and proud,
While mind, and heart,
Beats loud.

Flapping its wings,
Flying around, seeking,
Flowers flys a butterfly,
On a wall finally settling.
On a tree, a sparrow,
Hops from branch to branch,
A pigeon on the roof,
Readying for its launch.

9 798885 466554

Printed by Libri Plureos GmbH in Hamburg,
Germany